Is That A Real Man

In Your

Mirror?

By: Otha Morris

Order this book online at www.trafford.com
or email orders@trafford.com

Most Trafford titles are also available at major online book retailers.

Printed in the United States of America.

ISBN: 978-1-4669-9306-8 (sc)
ISBN: 978-1-4669-9307-5 (e)

Library of Congress Control Number: 2013908056

Trafford rev. 05/01/2013

 www.trafford.com

North America & international
toll-free: 1 888 232 4444 (USA & Canada)
fax: 812 355 4082

Acknowledgements

First I want to give all the honor and glory to God and His son; Jesus Christ, our Savior. Without them, me and none of this would be possible.

I want to recognize my wife Deborah, who has stood by be through thick and thin and encouraged me along every step of the way and I love her dearly.

I want to thank my granddaughter Olivia because without her keeping me up at night I couldn't have stayed up to write this book. She's Papa's Big Girl, but still his baby!

I want to recognize my children; Corey, Erin and Stephen for their inspiration to write this book, especially the young men and I hope that they can use something from this to better their lives.

I have to recognize my mother-in-law Ann who is really just like my mom. I want to thank her for all of her support, wisdom, guidance and advice.

Next is Aunt Charlotte whose support and much needed comedic thoughts were needed from time to time.

Finally there's you Adrienne. You know who you are and what you are to me aside from a co conspirator in our assault on 'Big Blackie'! Thank you for your much needed input and criticism when it was needed.

And for anyone who may feel left out, don't. You know what you've contributed and it may be on the inside.

I love you all and I want you all to go forward with Peace, Love and Understanding!

Preface

This book is to honor and praise the real men of the world and to those who hope to and want to attain that that status. There is no need to feel offended or feel belittled by what lies between the covers of this book. It is what it is; the truth. There are two things about the truth you need to know. First; the truth will always be the truth. Second the truth needs no defense.

The question that needs to be asked is: " How can you be a man if you've never seen or met a man?" Maybe you'll find the answer here, I truly hope so. I'll ask this question again later. So now that you've got your book, sit back, get comfortable and take this ride. I hope it will be as enjoyable for you to read as it was for me to write. It may not do anything for you and then again it may do you some good.

If you can't afford to step up and be a man, then the cost of being you is too high!

Table of Contents

The young boy approached the group of guys who were casually shooting the breeze on the corner. As he entered their midst he asked: "Who's my daddy?"

Dumbfounded and startled none of them could TRUTHFULLY say: " I am". Not because none of them could acknowledge having fathered the child, but because there is a difference between being a father and being a daddy.

The child of a real man wouldn't have to ask that question because he wouldn't have to hunt his daddy down to find out who he is.

So guys take a look…. Is that a real man in your mirror?

" I'm starting with the man in the mirror, I'm asking him to change his ways.
No message could have been any clearer, if you want to make the world a better place, take a look at yourself and make a change!"
"Man in the Mirror"-By Michael Jackson

Men it's time to 'man up'. Stop using that old excuse that " the man is holding me back or holding me down".

Let's look at this logically. There is no way anyone can hold you back or down without being back there or down there with you.

Stop making excuses for not attaining your manhood and step up to the plate.

Chapter One

What Is A Man ?

Before we get started on this journey we first need to know what a man is supposed to be. Webster's Dictionary says a man is an ' adult male human being'. We all know that there is more to it than this. We all probably have different ideas about what it takes to be a man, however I'm talking about being 'A MAN' not trying to be 'THE MAN'.

Is a man the one who gets his butt up out of bed every morning, goes to work, comes home, spends time with his children if there are any, handles the bills or is smart enough to

give his wife the money to handle them
if that is not his forte and takes care of
his wife?

Or is he the one who tries to pull as
many women as he can, create
numerous children and doesn't provide
for them or his wife if there is one?
The one who only makes token
donations to the upkeep of his woman.
I said woman, not lady and that is
because there is a difference.

To me, the real man
takes care of his responsibilities, not let
his responsibilities take care of him.
The ones who are doing this know who
they are. Laying around the woman's
house, watching her television, eating
up the food that should be going to the
children.

Hanging
on the corner with the 'boys' and

waiting for HER check to arrive. Waiting for that check so they can grab whatever they can to put gas in their car. And it's funny they always seem to have a car. They also must buy some new 'threads' for the club tonight. These guys want to call themselves 'Players', but just hold on, I'll get to the 'Players' in a few.

The real men don't wait on her check, they bring the check into the house. The real men handle their business. And though they may be tired at the end of the day it doesn't deter them from getting up the next morning and doing it all over again.

A real man doesn't pretend that he needs a car to get to work. If he has a job he will get there. And he really doesn't want a job anyway. The real man wants an opportunity. A job may sustain him for a while, but that is not what he wants. A real man will usually develop the desire and concept of wanting more.

If you look at it realistically JOB only means 'Just Over Broke'! That says that when you get your paycheck and handle your responsibilities you have just enough money to make it through the week to the next paycheck. A real man can live like this for a while, but he's always looking for that one break or opportunity.

The others are not going out like that. All that hard work and nothing to show for it at the end of the week. The blind are not the only ones who cannot see; those who won't look at life or face reality makes this number at least three.

These guys want to hang out

on the block with the fellas. I told you that I would get to them. These are the 'Players'.

Why do they call themselves 'Players'? Is it because they think they can run some game on folks, especially women? Or is it because they love to play games, video and otherwise? The Bible says something about this. It says something like this even though it may not be quoted exactly you will get the message behind the words. It goes something like this: "When I was a child, I thought as a child. I played as a child. I did childish things. But when I became a man I put childish things away."

Now the only real players that I know of are still playing games. However these guys are getting paid to play, have endorsement deals and investments. Players on the corner aren't getting PAID for being there. They do however endorse different products every day and don't get dime one for lighting up that smoke or turning up that '40' or bottle of wine.

Companies pay to put these products on television, radio, billboards and posters. And here you are doing it for free! From where I stand I see Players getting played not paid! And not only that, these guys are probably not realizing that they are also destroying their bodies. One day this behavior is going to take them out and all you can say to the Players then is: GAME OVER"!

I need to get back to talking about the real men for a moment because these are the guys who are doing the right thing and know *where home is.*

To the real man home isn't just a place he hangs his hat, takes off his shoes and puts up his feet. Home is the place where he, his wife and children, if this applies live. Mind you there is a difference between living and existing.

To exist means to come into being or merely just being there. To live is to be alive; to maintain oneself, to have a life rich in experience and to remain in human memory or record.

Real men don't want to just be there. They want the world to know that they have been there. How is this possible? The first and most notable way is by becoming a father. Now don't get it twisted about becoming a father, because that does not make you a 'daddy'. These are two totally different things. Just about any man can father a child if he finds a woman that will go along with him and what he wants to do. By this I mean have sex with him. And even that has two sides to it. There is a big difference between having sex and making love, but we'll get to that a little later on.

You see, a lot of fathers make a child and then they're off. Off to the corner or to their next conquest. They have no thought or intention of providing any type of support: financial, emotional or spiritual to this child that they helped bring into this world.

A 'daddy' is a totally different creature. This man is going to be there for the child and the mother through thick and thin, hell and high water. He is going to get up and go to work. He will find some kind of employment just to be able to bring funds in to take care of mother and child. To take care of home. A real man will do without just so long as home is taken care of.

There may be times when he comes up short, but he will never give up, walk off and leave those who are depending on him to provide for them.

You may ask: " What about the woman or wife? Why can't she provide?" God didn't set it up that way. He created woman as a companion and 'help meet' not a 'help mate'. Check your Bible. It means that she is to meet her man with the help he may require if and when he falls short. There is no 50/50 split in this arrangement. So if you're going to be a real man then you need to know your *role.*

Whoever told you those myths about raising children, doing housework and all those things being done around the house was a woman's job was wrong! Not only is their game twisted, but their minds are too!

Are these not your children also? Don't you live there too? Well if you want your house be a home then you better man up and do the right thing. You want to live and let people know that you are living. Is there a better way than putting your family out front for all to see?

Now you Players, the ones who want to be 'the man', I don't want you to feel too bad about what I said concerning those real Players getting paid. Don't be fooled. The only difference between you and a lot of *them is those dollar ($) signs. A lot of them, even with all the money they make, I won't say can't, but just won't take care of home.*

I'm not the one to judge them, but can someone please explain to me this: How do you earn millions of dollars and get your sorry tail hauled into court for non-payment of a child support order?

Did you not know that you had to pay to play? Yes, she looked good, but that ten minutes of pleasure now costs you at least eighteen years of financial obligations.

This is where knowing the difference between having sex and making love comes into play. Having sex is just a physical act between two people where reproduction is sometimes, though rarely the intended result.

Most times there are no strings attached. No commitment. And sometimes no further involvement. This act is so common that creatures of the animal kingdom do it every day.

Making love is a totally different story. Yes it involves sex, but it goes to a totally different level. Making love is emotional. There is a commitment between two partners to each other. It just doesn't involve the act of having sex.

Making love requires intimacy, which is a very close contact, association and familiarity between the partners who are usually husband and wife. Why? Because the two are made one and I don't believe you can get any closer than that.

Let's get Biblical for a moment. Everyone knows or thinks they know the story of Samson and Delilah, but do they really? Everyone thinks that Samson just had it going on with this beautiful chick Delilah.

Samson and Delilah may have been getting down. Having sex. Committing fornication and adultery. However you may or may not know it, but Samson was married. He had a wife in another country. You Players know the story: a long way from home, lonely and horny. Waiting for the first opportunity to get with a woman. Contrary to lines from that old song that says: "If you can't be with the one you, love, love the one you're with". There are consequences for this attitude.

Well you see Samson wanted to and did have sex

with Delilah, but he wanted more. What he wanted more than sex was intimacy! He wanted someone he could talk to and confide in.

Why do you think it took so long for Delilah to get the secret about his strength? He had to be sure that she could be trusted. Look what happened to him.

He still got betrayed. Why? Because the one that he should have been confiding in was back home waiting faithfully. Sometimes you've got to pay to play and the price can be too high!

A lot of you guys will probably point to this example and say women can't be trusted. Don't put the blame on the women, check yourself out. Did you or did you not choose to go after that woman? She was probably somewhere minding her business and you rolled up with all sorts of con and game.

That's what Players do. Throw out some slick lines and hope that she'll fall for them. Some of you are so slick and smooth talking that the words roll off your tongue like butter. And by the time you're through talking you'll have some weak willed and weak minded young woman believing wrong is right!

Oh yeah, you're smooth. You're slick. You're a bad man. However when she flips the script on you now she's all kinds of B's and worse. Bro' she did what you did, only better. Don't hate the Player, learn the game!

Don't say women can't be trusted. Remember, you rolled up and chose her, so I guess there was something

wrong with your selection process.
Especially if you chose someone to play
your game, with your rules and you end
up losing The best advice that I can
give is for real men to take a stand!
The rest of you need to get a plan!

The Family Man

*"Papa was a rolling stone.
Wherever he laid his hat was his home.
And when he died all he left was us, all
alone." - The Temptations*

*So I ask: "Was Papa a real man or a
Player?"*

The Family Man

Now we come to the part of life that the Player doesn't want to have much or anything to do with. The family. Now family has many definitions, but let's go with this: a group of persons of common ancestry; a group of individuals living under one roof and under one head.

The family usually consists of a man with a wife and children dependent upon him, a responsible man of domestic habits.

Now I would like to know what part of the above applies to you

Players? If you guys are willing to admit it there isn't one statement here that applies to you. The guys on the corner or the block; they'll tell you that's their family right there surrounding them. They're with you at every turn, every move you make they're there.

These are your 'boys', 'homeys' or whatever and it doesn't get any tighter than that for you. Every now and then one of you may get struck by your conscience and drop by, usually empty handed to check on your children. This attack of conscience doesn't come often and doesn't last for any significant length of time.

What happened to the

responsible man of domestic habits? What of the dependent wife and children? Hell, you cats can't even live under the same roof with your dependents. You usually have to 'crash' with one of your partners and they're probably sponging off some woman and her children! And you call yourself a man?

Do any of you know what the family needs? Not that you're coming with it. Do you know where your children go to school? Better yet, do you know how old they are? Wait a minute, do you even know their names?

You guys don't have any family or friends. All you've got is some 'partners'. I hope that when it comes time to put you in the ground that you still have at least six of those partners, associates, acquantances or as you call them 'friends'. Remember there's six handles on that casket!

The real man, he's from a different cut. This is the man of responsibilities and domestic habits. He usually has a wife and children living with him under the same roof. We all know that there are some exceptions, but this man is still taking care of business.

He and the mother of the children may not still be hitting it off, however they are probably remaining sociable towards each other even if it's only for the sake of the children. After all, they didn't ask to be here.

This man knows his children and I'm not just talking about knowing their names. He knows their ages and birthdays. He knows where they go to school, who their playmates are, what they like and don't like. Daddy knows where they hang out and what time they're in the house.

As I said before, most any male can be a father, but it takes a special man to be a 'daddy'! Daddy knows what it's like to get up in the middle of the night with a sick child and stay up all night. He knows how to go into the childs' bedroom and get the monster out of the closet or from under the bed.

Daddy knows how to go into the kitchen and throw some concoction together and try and pass it off as a 'gourmet meal'. Dad, he's that guy who slips you a few extra bucks so you can go to the movies or arcade. He's also the one who wants to know and will know everything about this guy who has come calling on his daughter. Daddy may want to know as far back as to when this young man's ancestors first came to this country!

Daddy is truly a unique creature. A big, warm 'Teddy Bear' who will turn into a 'Grizzly' on you in no time flat. If you don't believe it then try messing with one of his children. Please don't let it be one of his girls because if you know like I know, your heart and soul will belong to God, but your a_ _ belongs to daddy!

Let's talk about the relationship that he has with the mother; usually his wife. No, I'm not going to say that he should put her up on a pedestal. However if that's where he feels she should be then so be it. Who are you and I to say she doesn't deserve to be up there? Anyway, the man is going to take care of his better half if he is a man.

He's going to make sure that she has what she needs and then some. He's not going to be jealous or suspicious of her and what she does. He's going to allow her to be a lady and that's something you Players know nothing about.

Why do I say this? You cats don't know the difference between a woman and a lady. Allow me to break it down for you. A woman is merely an adult female. Whereas a lady is a woman that has proprietary rights or authority. She receives homage or devotion from her husband or lover. She is a woman of refinement and gentle manners. Those are some of the differences. Well Players, who do you know?

Do you tell the guys: " I was out with my woman" or do you say: " I was out with my lady"? And here's some food for thought: do you really know which you were out with?

From where I sit she could be your woman and then flip the script and be someone else's woman later on that same night. Players! You ain't the only ones that got or play games!

A real man doesn't worry about these sort of things with his lady. He knows what she's about because he knows what he's about. I say this because God says they become one flesh. The right hand may not know what the left hand is doing, because it can make a fist without letting the left know what's going on.

They have to move in unison and that is what a man and his lady do. With them it's a joint effort in most situations. It's usually a 'we' thing because most things are done together. It's been said that: " We all can't talk at the same time, but we can sing together". That's what they do, sing together, harmonize. That's what it takes.

Oh yeah, Players I didn't mean to hurt your feelings or throw you off your game by saying your woman may also be someone else's woman. And if I did who cares? You being the Player that you are it shouldn't really matter to you anyway. It may be a fact, but don't dwell on that. Let me leave you with this down to earth fact: You can't miss what you can't measure! Think on it.

Now back to dad. Daddy is there when his child takes his ir her first steps, when they speak or utter their first words, on the first day of school and when they first fall off their bikes. He knows when the first tooth comes in or out. Yeah that's 'daddy'. Those are things that players know nothing about.

When you can sit up all night with a sick child and still get your butt up and go to work with no sleep, knowing that you're probably coming home to a similar situation, then you've done something.

Daddy realizes that mom has had to spend all day dealing with this and she is probably tired and in need of some rest and down time. Dad doesn't hesitate to step in and step up. When they say: " Man up!" this is what they're talking about.

You've got to turn your attention to the needs of others and basically forget about what you want to do. If fathers set this kind of examples for their sons then maybe we wouldn't have as many young men lost to the streets. There is no guarantee, but it's a step in the right direction. Sometimes no matter how hard a father tries, the sons will go astray. You can show them the right path to follow, but somewhere along the way, every now and then they will stray from the path.

However if any of what you've taught them stuck, they'll come back. If they don't, then you can't beat yourself up over it. The old saying: " You can lead a horse to water, but you can't make him drink" applies here.

These young men are like the rest of us; imperfect. They possess free will and are able to make choices on their own. This is the very thing that got Adam in trouble in the garden of Eden. Just wouldn't listen. Had to do it his way. We all see how that turned out because we're still paying for his choice!

Dads, don't let the choices of your sons make you pay. Yes you love them, but that's on them. Let them deal with the consequences of their actions or inactions. Sometimes not doing is just as bad or worse than actually participating.

This pretty much has been a talk about fathers and sons. Mothers, ladies, women and daughters, please don't feel slighted. It went this way for a reason.

Men are supposed to take the lead role in the family. Unfortunately that's not the case too often or we wouldn't have so many single parent households headed up by the mother. I said: "so many", not all. Don't get it twisted. There are many single parent households headed up by the father. I salute these brothers for taking a stand and deciding to be a man.

Players are not cut from this cloth. How does it go? "If you ain't gonna pee, get off the pot"! Players ain't gonna pee, so you'll never find them anywhere near the pot!

Mother's you just keep on doing what you're doung. And the same goes for you; every mother is not a 'mommy'. Think about it , but don't sweat it yet. This is about the men.

Family is a very long and complicated topic. We couldn't cover it all in these pages so I just touched lightly on some of it's aspects with the hope that I could wake up some sleeping minds and praise others.

Men take note: the family, your family is important. How and where they end up is largely in your hands. Can you and will you handle it?

Friends

*" They smile in your face, but all the
they want to take your place…"*
'Backstabbers' - by The O'Jays

Friends

Now let's talk about something that should be of interest to all; 'friends'. Friend as Mr. Webster describes him is:' one attached to another by affection or esteem'.

Let's start with the real man. If you notice and look real close this man does not have a lot of friends if any at all. The first and most important friend of a real man should be his wife or significant other.

This person should be able to be confided in with a man's innermost thoughts, ideas, secrets and dreams with the knowledge that it will go no further than them. Any person beyond this one a man would really have to ask himself: "Can I trust this person"?

There are many men out there that have had to learn the hard way that their 'boys' are not their friends. When I say this one young man comes to mind. A lot of you know of him. He was a young rapper that came out of Philadelphia.

He caught on and was on the road to fame and fortune. So what did he do? He tried to bring his boys along for the ride. All they did was bring the brother down, almost to nothing.

However he learned from that experience and with the help from G0od and some hard work and sound advice he recovered and made it to the top of his profession.

Not just as a rapper, but as a notoriously big time actor who is in high demand in Hollywood. If you take the lessons that are put before you then sometimes a setback will only be a setup for a greater comeback!

This young man learned the hard truth in the saying that: "Everybody that comes with you can't go with you"! That's true because at some point a man is going to have to go his way and he may need to travel alone for a time until he can find that real friend.

The Players or the ones who want to be 'the man', they have a totally different outlook on friends. To these guys they've got their boys, their posse or entourage. If they would just step back and look they would see that these guys are nothing but 'hangers on'. They are just there to see what they can get or what you will bring to the table.

Do really think that you can tell your innermost thoughts to this group? If you do it will be on the street before the morning newspaper comes out or before the evening news comes on that night.

If all you guys are doing is hanging on the corner you can do better. They say: "Misery loves company". Players, come alive. You can do better. And if you can't, you can do bad by yourself! You don't need to sit around and participate in the 'pity party'.

If you have the chance to get off the corner and improve your station in life I suggest that you take it. Don't fall for the 'crab barrel syndrome' and let the crabs keep pulling you back into the barrel when you try to climb out.

There are too many brothers out there with so much talent and untapped potential. There are guys out there right now who could put some NBA players to shame on the court. Ever hear of Earl Manigault? Herman "The Helicopter'? Probably not, but these are just two playground legends that would have been great in the NBA if they didn't let little things hold them back.

Why don't guys such as these make their mark? They don't because they settled for what someone told them what their station in life was supposed to be so don't try and rise above it. It's not true.

Most of you Players can stop playing if you really want to. You can be real men if you choose to be. If you have a dream you need to make it into a goal. Once you have a goal all you need to do is form a plan to get you to that goal.

Now along the way you will encounter obstacles. People or things are going to get in your way. People will doubt you, but you have to keep on pushing. You may have to change or alter your plan to attain your goal, but never change your goal. Keep your eyes on the prize.

Now if the guys that you're hanging with can't help you attain your goal, can't offer any positive reinforcement for your plans or just can't applaud your effort, do you need them? Are they really your friends? I think not.

They may say to you: "You know I'm your friend brother because if anything goes down I got your back!

I'm there for you"! If you are a real man you won't be put in a position where someone needs to 'have your back'.

It's been said that : "You are where you are today because of the choices you made yesterday". What choices did you make yesterday? Looking at today, would you change any of yesterday's choices?

When all is said and done how many friends do you really have? What you may have is many acquaintances. Now these you may need. At least six anyway. One for each handle on your casket! So choose your friends very carefully because I'll bet those that came with you don't want to go on that trip.

SEX: Is Not A Spectator Sport

*" A man's got to know his
limitations."*
Clint Eastwood
'Magnum Force'

Sex Is Not A Spectator Sport

Now comes what a lot of you guys have been waiting to hear about. Then again it may be something you really don't want to hear about. Sex.

Sex has it's good side, especially when used as God intended. It also has it's bad or dark side and that is what we are going to explore first.

All men think about sex. From the alcoholic or junkie in the street to the so called most holy of holy men. If they say they don't then they're lying and the truth isn't in *them.*

You can lie to me and other people, but there are three that can't lie to; God, the devil and yourself. So let's be real about this. I don't care if the men are in their seventies or eighties they still have the thought or desire even though the ability may no longer be there.

The bad or dark side: Let's take a look at what has been going on with these priests, preachers, clergy and the young men that they are supposed to be mentoring or teaching.

The biggest reason that they are all over these young men is because they are so easily accessible. They are young, innocent and too trusting. Being left alone with a person of this magnitude and position lets one believe that whatever this person tells them is right. The females or young ladies of the church are rarely put in these situations because they don't have these types of roles in the church as either a follower or leader.

We've got the same problem with teachers. The biggest difference is that now we have both male and female predators. I see where the men are going after these young womeis really sick and disgusting, but when the female teachers start going after young men I really think they have a worse problem!

Why? Are you and I supposed to

believe that a woman is really going to have a problem getting a man to have sex with her? As one comedian says: "Women are offered sex as much as twenty times a day". If women could look beyond the surface they could see that a simple act of holding a door for them is an invitation to have sex. But this isn't for the women so let's get back to where we need to be. Some of the worst uses of sex is done by the pedophiles. With these creatures there is no emotionor feeling for the other person involved. It's usually a forced situation by use of sheer strength or a weapon. The weapon doesn't have to be a physical one. It could be emotional or verbal. A mere threat could scare a child into doing something they really don't want to do. A child may also want to please the adult that is pressing the issue. This is nothing less than Rape!

Why does a person do this? Who knows? They may be feeling bad about themselves and their inadequacies and feel the need to lash out at someone. They may want to make a statement so they can feel better about themselves and their pitiful, miserable existence.

All of this is bad and there is probably a lot more to talk about here, but I must move on.

Let's touch on you Players out there. Could it be that you are called 'Players' because youthink *this is a game and you feel the need to keep score? Yes you do. How many times do you come back to the 'boys' and relate your latest conquest whether it be the truth or a lie?*

Who are you guys trying to fool or impress besides yourself? You come back and tell all the sordid details, real or fictional with the latter usually being more realistic. You say what she did to you and what you did to her. You tell that fantastic lie about how you went all night long and how you let her all tired and wore out.

Player, Player. I applaud you on that fantastic imagination that you possess. However a real man doesn't have to kep score on the number of women he's been with because that's personal. So why do you feel that your 'boys' have a right to know?

If you were real men, instead of bragging on your exploits and especially your endurance, you might want to take this little tidbit of knowledge for the truth that it is: "She will always be able to look up longer than you can look down"!

For a real man sex takes on a whole different light. First of all it was given by God primarily for procreation. Pleasure was an after thought.

When being used for pleasure it

takes on a totally different dimension, something we like to call 'making love'. This is different than everything mentioned before mainly because there is an emotional attachment between the partners which occasionally results in children.

After a man and woman make love they don't run out to the 'boys' or 'girls' and brag and tell what happened. They don't have to because it's no one else's business. It's a private matter between two individuals that usually have not only an emotional attachment, but a legak one(marriage) also. What they do in their bedroom is between them and God. No spectators allowed!

Spectators! You are the guys sitting on the sidelines waiting to get all the juicy details. Hearing all about what someone else did. What good does it do you? You may as well go home, watch television or read a book. Those stories at least have the appearance of reality even though I hope you realize that they're not.

Wait! Here's a novel idea. Why not get yourself into a committed relationship of your own and have your own stories to keep to yourself? Oh, I forgot, you're a Player. You have to report back to the 'boys' so you can compare stories.

Wolves runin packs. I wonder if

the males get together and discuss who they've been with. I don't think so. So why do you? Are these animals on a higher plane than you, even though you dom have a lot of similarities? The most notable likeness is that you both run in packs and neither have any emotional ties to the female of your species.

Before I forget, all you pastors, preachers and priests, don't show up on television screen crying and confessing your sins as another minister did. Crying and asking God and man to forgive you for the wrong that you've done.

First of all the forgiveness from man is superficial and doesn't carry much weight except to you. Someone may say that they forgive you, but they don't forget what you've done. However God saw you when you were doing what you were doing and He will forgive you. Besides you don't really want any forgiveness from man anyway. What you want is a chance to parlay dirty deeds into a big payday! It's been done time and time again.

You get up in front of the congregation, confess your sins, ask for forgiveness and pass the collection plate. It seems to me if you really wanted to cash in you should have filmed it, made yourself some bootleg copies nd sold them on the street unless you really wanted to go big time and sell them to the porn industry. Since it's all about the mighty dollar you may as well be the star and get paid in full!

However that may not be too good of an idea. You see if you go public with what you've done to those children you will land in jail or prison. And if that is where you land you may really become a star! Just picture the whole cell block lining up to see you.

Boy I'm glad real men don't have to go out like this, putting all therir business out there on front street. The real man makes his business just that; his business. He doesn't need an audience, forgiveness or approval from anyone for his sexual activity. Why?

Because what he's doing is the right thing. I's his thing, not his and his partners'. It doesn't concern or involve anyone else except his mate and that's the way it should be.

All you brothers that are on the 'down low', if that's the wy you want to roll that's on you. However as the saying goes: "You can pay now or pay later"! Anyway you slice it, you are going to pay.

Whatever is done in the dark is going to come to the light. So if your boys don't know now they sure as hell will know at some time in the future. And whenthey find out you may need to regroup and find another six for those casket handles and you may need them sooner than *you originally anticipated!*

I can say one thing about that pack of wolves……I know that they aren't going out like that, so how can you? What are you guys thinking? It doesn't matter who's pitching and who's catching, this game is all wrong and I know that it's not the only game in town. Then again, you are Players and this is how you roll.

Players tell me this: Where do you see yourself fitting into God's overall plan? We already know that you're not going to Heaven, but where do you think you and this behavior is going to fit in on earth? This is food for some serious thought and you really should be eating.

When you come up with one of those sexually transmitted diseases(STD) don't blame God. Just look in the mirror and ask yourself: How could you and what were you thinking? You were playing in the devil's casino, playing his game and just like the casinos the dealer (Satan) doesn't pay for any mistakes. It's like getting 22 in Blackjack or rolling 'snake eyes' on the dice table. YOU LOSE!

If you guys still insist on making this a game and feel that you need an audience just keep on doing what you're doing. Keep score all you want, but no matter what numbers you come up with you're still going to lose. The audience you get may *not be the one you want and chances are you won't even know that they are there.*

Real men, I don't need to tell you, but I'm going to say it anyway: Take a stand. Don't allow your family to even think about walking or experimenting with the dark side. Keep your sons off the street corners even if he's only hanging with his friends. That's how it starts. Don't allow it. Make him get a goal and help him plan how to get to it. Encourage him and give assistance whenever you feel he needs it or asks for it. Most of all show him how to be a man.

"Money, Oh Money...Got To My Hands On Some!" by The Fatback Band

"It's better to have it and not need it, than to need it and not have it!"
Richard Pryor- 'Carwash'

" Money, Oh Money…. Got To Get My Hands On Some" -The Fatback Band

Here we go with another favorite topic of all Players…..MONEY! It's been said that money is the root of all evil. I respectfully disagree. If you go back to the beginning of mans existence you will see that it was disobedience, but we're talking about money so let's get back to it.

If you look closely you will find that not money, but the lack of it causes a lot more of the trouble in the world today. That's not saying that having money doen't cause problems, because most of the people with it are always trying to figure out ways to get more of it. Those without are trying to find ways to get it and a lot of time it leads to a life of crime and that takes them someplace they really don't want to be or go to.

We can touch on drugs, prostitution, stealing and such, but let me give you this one thing to think about…..greed! I'm almost willing to bet that if I went into any church; supposedly a place of love for your fellow man and one another. I believe that I could go into a church with a congregation of one hundred people, throw $10,000 in one dollar bills into the air, and *there would be some people that wouldn't get a dollar!*

Why? Because these folks are going to do whatever it takes to get as much as they can. They will push children aside, walk all over the elderly and do what they've got to do to get it. This is the church, so what do you think is going to happen in the streets?

How many of you Players are on the corner slinging your nickel and dime bags of whatever to make a dollar? You've convinced yourself that this is your hustle, a chance to make some change. You justify what you're doing by saying that you've got to make a living. You can fool yourself all you want, but you're the only one that you are fooling.

Why make some change when you can make some dollars? So instead of looking for and finding a job you aspire to move up from street level; the corner dealer,to a bigger and more lucrative position.

Now you want to be a distributor and have guys working the corners for you. Did it ever occur to you that the higher you go the more jail or prison time you expose yourself to when you get caught? And eventually you will get caught. All that money you made will just go to the government and they may not say it, but they will politely thank you for all the time and work you in to provide them with cash, cars, jewelry, real estate and anything else you may have acquired.

When you're out there on the corner and you see all those cats driving by in their hot cars, the jewelry, the 'bling-bling', the rolls of cash and the women; I said women not ladies. You say to yourself: "I want some of that"! I'll bet you do, but let me give you this little morsel of knowledge. The devil always pays you or gives you your reward up front, before you put any real work in.

He'll come back to collect on what he's given you later on. When? You'll never know, but he is coming to collect! Some of you say that you don't worry about getting caught. You can do the time. You're hard. You're a bad man. A couple of things here; first of all you don't have to make the time. The time is already made, all you have to do is outlive your share of it that the judge gave you.

You say you're hard? You want to be hard? Get a job and go to work every day. Provide food, clothing and shelter for your children. Take care of your lady. Be someone that can be looked to instead of for. These are a few ways to be hard, but not all of them. If you can't do these things you're not hard, you're more like 'Silly-Putty'.

Prostitution. It is said to be the oldest profession in the world. And what is it really? It's the sale of the body for a price, be it money or some other commodity. We usually associate this act with women, but men participate even though they usually are the 'buyers'.

Two things guys; First: If you had a wife you wouldn't have to go out like this. Second: if your game was as good as you think or say it is, you wouldn't be going into your pockets! Player? I don't think so.

You brothers ought to get real about what you're doing. Did it ever occur to you that this woman is someone's daughter or sisyter? Hell, she may even be someone's mother! And I know that you have at least one of the aforementioned.

How would you feel knowing that your sister or daughter was going outlike that? What if it was one of your boys off the corner getting with her? How would you feel? Stupid angry or both? What would you do to rectify the situation?

We know what a real man would do without saying, even though we will later on. What would you the player do? You gonna just sit there and let it continue? Will you confront or jump on your boy? Talk to your sister or daughter? Or will you just use that standard old line: " That's them"! If you don't step up to the plate and do something to change what's going down, then who in hell do you think is going to respect you?

To the rest of your boys you ain't

nothing but a punk and they'll be waiting next in line for her. The sad thing about this whole ordeal for you is that you're not making any money out of it unles you're acting as the pimp.

Some lines from the old movie 'The Mack' say: "Pimping is big business. It's been going on since the beginning of time. Just remember; a pimp is only as good as his product. Any man can control a woman's body. You've got to be able to control her mind"!

So are you the pimp? Let me tell you this: Your product ain't hitting on too much! Why do I say this? Aren't you still out there on the corner? Your station in life has not changed one bit. You're no better off and most times not as good as a wino. A wino is only worried about running out of wine. However he will find a way to make some money to get that next bottle even if it means 'churching up' with some buddies. He will get that bottle.

What are you doing? Still waiting around for a woman to make a way for you. It's time for you players to step up and grow up, but since it's so hard maybe I should liken you to a jellyfish. I say a jellyfish because like you, a jellyfish ain't got no backbone! Pardon the use of a double negative in the sentence, but that's how I need to come across to reach some folks at times.

I'm coming down so hard on you Players because I know that you can do better. If you would, this world we live in would change greatly and more than likely for the better. Remember what I said about all those 'could be' ballplayers that are in the playgrounds?

Well how many 'could be' statesmen do we have on those corners? There are plenty of intelligent ideas being kicked around on those corners when they should be heard in a larger arena. There are some ideas out there that would turn Wall Street up on it's end.

More than likely the national

debt could be erased if it were left in the hands of some guys on the corner. They know that you can't spend what you don't have in your pocket. It's not a hard concept to understand. The solution may be on your corner.

Players I've been coming down on you guys pretty hard, but there is a reason for this. I don't necessarily want you to come around to my way of thinking, but I do want you to think about what you're doing and how you're living.

Let's talk about the men with some serious money. I'm talking about obscene amounts of cash. Money that most of us don't even dream about having.

First let us make the distinction between being rich and being wealthy. Believe me, there is a difference. Let's look at a professional ballplayer, say a player for the Los Angeles Lakers. All of those ballplayers make millions of dollars and that is some serious money. These guys are rich. They are making those ends. They're rich, but not wealthy.

You want to know who's wealthy? The man who is paying all those salaries. He's the one who's wealthy. Look at this on the real side. This man, usually the team owner has numerous expenses besides paying his players.

All the coaches and scouts have to be paid. Don't forget the trainers and office staff. Think about the arena costs and how many people have to be paid to run and maintain it especially on game days. How well do you think you could live off the money he pays just for utilities?

These owners have to reach into their pockets to pay for team transportation, food, lodging and insurance of various natures. This list goes on and on. So if you never knew the difference between the two; rich and wealthy, now you do.

We're not going to waste time on the wealthy men because you rarely hear of them doing anything stupid or foolish where their money is concerned. The rich are creatures of a different cut.

Don't get me wrong, some men attain the money that they only used to dream about and put it to use like someone that has had it all their lives. They act like they have some sense and are used to having things.

These brothers don't need to be talked to much either. It's my other brothers, whether you be black, white, yellow, red or whatever that I need to talk to. Before I go there it has dawned on me that there is another group I really and truly need to address.

A popular radio personality ran a segment on his show entitled:

'Pimps in the Pulpit". By the title you should already know where I'm about to go. The Church!

If we really wanted to clear up the national debt all we would have to do is put the Church on the stock market. What? Oh, you didn't know? The Church is the largest money making institution in America. On top of all that they are all exempt from paying taxes.

If all the churches got together they could close down the banking industry. Am I crazy? Check this out. If all church members closed their bank accounts and deposited them in a banking system established by the churches how many depositors would commercial banks have?

However it will never happen, not in this system of things that we have on this earth. The reason? As with most matters dealing with money......GREED! Someone is always going to want more and feel that they are legitimately entitled to a larger piece of the pie. Don't forget that, but let's move on to these wannabe preachers.

You guys are supposed to be workers for God, but let's face it, most of you are in it for the money. Instead of salvation you see dollar signs. Why do you pass the plate so many times during service? It's supposed to be an offering plate, but you've made it into a collection plate. Why count the money and then come back and ask for some more to get a nice round figure?

It's almost as if that when service is over, you take the money to a back room, throw it in the air and say: "What God wants He'll take. The rest belongs to me"!

At least be truthful to yourself even if you're not going to be honest with the congregation. God? You can't lie to or hide from Him. He already knows what you're all about, YOU. He knows exactly what you're doing.

I've never seen so many Gospel singers want to turn and be preachers and pastors like I do nowadays. Now you want to double-dip. You want to get paid for singing praises to God and talking about Him and His word too.

When you get up to preach the word you only say enough to make the people feel good and tickle their ears enough so that they'll come back next time and drop that cash into the plate. You get up there supposedly bringing the word of God and the whole time you're probably counting heads trying to anticipate how much money you'll take in.

You ain't doing nothing but trying to sell your speech or so called sermon. How dare you sell the word of God? If you sell this then you'll sell anything including things that you don't own such as your soul.

I don't know what you call it, but I say that you're just 'Pimping' your congregation. You just want them to bring in the money.

I say that you're pimping them because a lot of you live in big, fine houses and own two or three more. You have three, four, five cars and that fat bank account. Meanwhile you have members in your church that don't even have their lights on.

You however expect them to show up Sunday morning and still make a contribution to the church and you.

I'm going to get off you 'men' now, but only because there are more fish to fry and I need to get to them while the grease is still hot! Before I go, let me leave you 'Holy men' with this: "It's a fearful thing to fall into the hands of the living God"!

Remember back in the day when you were in high school and the girls told you that they couldn't get with you for one or all of these three reasons; youm didn't have any money, any class and no future?

Well you showed them didn't you? You're that professional athlete now and what do you do? You have the money so now you have to go out and buy, but you buy too excessively. Can someone please explain to me the logic of building a 25,000 square foot home with more bayhrooms than bedrooms when you are a single unattached young man? Who in the hell are you trying to impress?

You may have grown up poor and without many luxuries, but I know that you ate. Don't act like a hungry man at a free buffet. Act as though you've seen food and that you have eaten recently.

Don't let your cash run out the way the food at the buffet table does. In case you hadn't noticed, someone is always refilling the trays on the buffet table, but who will be refilling your wallet?

I don't know, maybe it's just me, but can someone please tell me or explain to me rationally how it's possible for you to earn ten to twenty million dollars a year, for let's say eight years and then be broke inyear ten? You cats come come up with some of the dumbest ways to blow money that I have ever sen or heard of.

You young guys blow it on your friends and the guys that you grew up with. I told you before that everybody that comes with you can't go with you. Check yourself. Then of course, that player mentality that you had suppressed for so long because you didn't have the cash or means to support it resurfaces.

Now you can get the women. You know the ones who had looked

past you and clowned you. Again, I said women not ladies, please remember the difference. You've got the cash, you've got the women and now you've got to have the sex. Oh yeah, you do. And your dumb behind is so stupid you don't even consider any type of protection so if you don't end up with a STD you end up with a CHILD!

Well you ain't trying to get married, you've got too much playing to do. So now you've got to kick out child support. I've got news for you buddy, it's not going to be two or three hundred dollars a month. You're going to have to give up a percentage of your salary. That payment is going to be due for the next eighteen years! How many of *you do youm think will have aplaying career or even a contract for that long? Better invest wisely because those payments won't stop being due.*

You're living large man. Got a car for each day of the week and two for Sunday. House so large you can go for weeks and never go into some rooms. If your brain was that big you would be asking yourself: "What am I doing"? If your heart was that big you would consider doing something for the less fortunate and do it without all the media hoopla.

Some of these things are fine, in moderation. Don't get caught up in the hype that bigger is better especially when you don't need big. I'm tired of reading about some former star athlete who through poor money management, bad advice, spending to excess and being too generous, especially to women and so called friends has gone from the PENTHOUSE to the OUTHOUSE. Now the brother is vying for a spot under some bridge, in an alley or doorway. Just doesn't make any sense.

So you can look at money as the cause or contributor for many things good and bad. No matter what is said though, it's always better to have it and not need it, than to need it and not have it!

Education: What Do I Need Or Want?

A mind is a terrible thing to waste,
but what about a life?

Education: What Do I Need Or Want?

"I graduated from the College of the Streets. Got a Ph.D in how to make ends meet! Inflation in the nation doesn't bother me, 'cause I'm a scholar with a dollar as you can plainly see!" - From "The Dude" by Quincy Jones.

This little gem of wordology may appear to work for some, but not for many. I kind of thought that most men and Players alike would want more than just making 'ends meet'. If that's all you want then you don't want to live, you're content just existing.

How important is education and how much do you need?   Well that is going to depend on you and what you want out of life. I know that you've heard the line about going to school, get good grades, get a job and you can get anything that you want. Don't believe the hype surrounding this logic. Why not?

Look at all those college graduates out there that are not working in the fields they went to school and studied so hard for. Now look at all those graduates that can't even get a job flipping hamburgers at McDonalds. There's got to be another way besides going into a life of crime, so check this out.

Let's say that your dream is to own a 75 foot yacht. How do you get it? You've been to school, got the good grades, ot the job and still you can't find a way to get it. So what do you do? Do you give up on your dream? No! You've done all the prerequisites that were laid out to you early in life; school, grades and job. So what's left?

I told you earlier that you never change your goal or dream. I believe that I told you that job stood for 'Just Over Broke'. What you need to do is change or alter your *plan to attain your goal.*

Try this. If you want a 75 foot yacht, first you find someone who has one. When you find this person hopefully they will talk to you and after engaging this person in conversation, ask him how he went about getting his yacht.

Seems like a plan to me. I mean rationally speaking, what better way to find out how to acquire something besides asking someone who has what you want how they got theirs.

Now maybe what they went through to get theirs won't work for you, but there is someone out there that has a plan that will work for you. Plan your work and then work your plan.

How much education do you really need? Who knows exactly? However I do know this; it's best to know how to read and write at least on the tenth grade level and be able to count to twenty without taking off your shoes and socks.

Education is a wonderful thing, but it's not the only thing. Don't become an educated fool; so smart when it comes to book learning, but dumb as a rock when it comes to the streets and the real world. Face it, I don't care how learned you think you are, sooner or later you're going to have to go outside into the real world.

What your book lesrning didn't

teach you is that the real world that's outside your door will chew you up and spit you out like you were a bad meal. It don't know you and don't care anything about you.

Being educated doesn't just mean school learning. You've also got to take in the ways of the world and then find your own unique balance of the two. Find out what works for you and get in where you fit in.

Being scholastically educated doesn't necessarily mean that you will attain financial success. Some make their wealth on their athletic prowess and talent alone. Some scholars do make it, but athletes usually make it to their financial dreams a lot quicker. As for holding on to it, that can be quite a different story as I laid out before.

You have to find out what's right for you. You can't live someone else's dream that they have for you. If you try you will only become miserable and frustrated. Do your own thing so when all is said and done at least you will have done it your way. If what you choose to do makes you happy that's all that counts.

Those other people, you don't have to see them all the time, but you've got to be with you 24/7 and you can't change that. Don't be afraid to dream big. Dream that yacht, not a rowboat. Even if youend up in the rowboat at least you're in the water and you're headed in the right direction. Yes you may be disappointed, but at least you did try.

Nothing beats a try, but a failure. All failing should do is to inspire you to get right back up and try again. Just because you get knocked down doesn't mean you have to stay down. Don't get counted out and don't take a standing eight count. Get back in there and keep on punching until you knock all opposition to your dream out.

Who am I talking to? A real man should and probably already knows this and is still swinging. It's all you

Players and the few men that are a little bit lost that need this boost. You need to establish your dream so that you can improve your station in life.

Now if your content where you are then so be it. Just don't come around later in life whining and crying about how bad life has treated you. Life didn't do it, you did. All you had to do is want to really live and have a life. It was right there in front of you all the time. Don't start the pity party, there won't be any real men or ladies coming to it. After all, what do you have to offer that would make them want to take time off from whatever they could be doing to come and watch you wallow in your self pity?

Wake up! It's time to get a move on. Ben Franklin (He's the one that you're talking about in your quest for the 'Benjamins') said it best when he said: "Lost time is never found again".

Stop looking for it, it's gone. You better start looking ahead so you can get ahead. Graduate from the streets only and see just how far it gets you. Put them both together and have a life.

My God Is Alive; Sorry About Yours!

Eternity: Smoking or Non- Smoking Since God is alive.... What in hell do you want?

Spirituality

"**By oneself evil is done. By oneself evil is left undone. Purity and impurity are personal concerns; no one can purify another**".

Author unknown

Spirituality

I'm not about to call your faith or religious beliefs and practices into question. I just want to make you aware of your existence and hope that you realize that you didn't get here on your own.

I know that there is a higher power than me and that He is the reason for my being. You can say that you don't believe in God or any higher or divine authority, but you're lying. You believe in something or someone.

I'm not about to tell you to clean up your life. Can't do it. Too much going on in my backyard to worry about yours, but I must admit, I did look over your fence and I saw aq few things that may be out of sorts.

Anyway, before I go there let me tell you a story. Actually it comes from my former pastor and it was told quite a few years ago so I will be updating it and adding to it a bit.

Since most men and I know all you Players are into sports you all should be able to follow along, understand and relate to this because it is about a game. A baseball game specifically that features two pretty unique teams with each having some very interesting players. The title is 'The Homerun Hitter With A Bloody Bat'.

I will assume that at sometime in your lives you have heard of some of the most prolific homerun hitters in the game of baseball. When you talk about homeruns, names such as Babe Ruth, Willie Mays and Mickey Mantle come to mind. Those are names for some of the more knowledgeable and elder followers of the game.

Some of you younger guys know names like Hank Aaron, Sammy Sosa, Mark Mcguire and Bobby Bonds. Some may want to throw Alex Rodriguez into the mix, fine.

In his era Babe Ruth was the man. He remained as such with the single season homerun mark of sixty until 1961 when Roger Maris, who came from nowhere and hit 61 homeruns.

No matter, 'The Babe' still held the career mark with 714 blasts. It couldn't stand. When no one was looking or paying attention, Hank Aaron quietly eased up on Ruth's record and broke it. Hank retired after hitting 755 homeruns, totally annihilating Babe's mark.

Then came the so called 'steroid'

era. Mark McGuire and Sammy Sosa made grand assaults on the single season record, both surpassing it, with Sosa doing it more than once and pushing Maris back in the history books.

Then again, when no one was paying attention, Bobby Bonds made his assault on the record books. When all was said and done Barry stood alone atop the homerun world with a single season mark of 73 homeruns and a career mark of 762 homeruns.

You can take this next statement any way you want, but here it is. You know that those statistics were not going to be left alone. Two Black men with the highest homerun totals in history? In America's so called favorite pastime? I don't care how progressive we say we are it wasn't going to happen or go down like that.

Someone says that Bonds was cheating. He was using performance enhancing drugs! Let me say this, it doesn't matter what drug he was or wasn't using! Why? The drugs supposedly make you stronger. So what does that have to do with hand and eye coordination? You still must have those to hit the ball. You wannabe judges of morality who reside in Congress, you need to leave those young interns alone and get off Barry too!

These are all great homerun hitters, but the one that I'm going to tell you about is greater than all of those combined. He's a homerun hitter and He's got a bloody bat. So let's get down to it.

Everyone knows the game of baseball. It's a game with nine players on each team. The objective is to score more runs or send more men around the bases and across home plate than your opponent. In order to score you must first come to bat at home plate, get to first base, advance to second and third bases and cross home plate before three outs are made.

Now this game like all games has rules. However if you play in this game you have to play by God's rules.

Rule one: Pray without ceasing. Not just on Sunday, but Monday, Tuesday, Wednesday, Thursday, Friday and Saturday too! Praying once a week makes one weak!

You can pray anywhere; while brushing your teeth, while driving down the street, while on your job. Anywhere! You don't have to move your lips to pray either. Real prayer ia an attitude of your heart. If your attitude isn't right you're not praying anyway. I don't care what you say with your lips, your heart has to be right. And when your heart is right God will hear you and come to your rescue. He may not come when you want Him to, but whenever He gets there it will be on time!

Rule two: You've got to believe that God's grace is sufficient. You can't be saved or earn eternal life by your own efforts or grace. None of us is worthy to be saved, but God's grace is sufficient enough to save us. Grace is something that is unmerited, you can't earn it, you can't buy it and you can't work better than someone else to get it.

You must have faith in God. God gives you His grace and grace saves you. Grace got us up this morning and started us on our way. Grace will make you love your enemies and grace will brighten your day. You've got to believe that God's grace is sufficient.

Third: You've got to love your enemies. If you can't love your enemies you can't play on the team. Somebody is gonna do you wrong, they're gonna rub you the wrong way. They're gonna talk about you, gonna criticize you.

Jesus said: "You have heard love your neighbor and hate your enemy, but I say to you if you want to play on my team you've got to love your enemies!"

You've got to do good to them that hate you. You've got to pray for them that despitefully use you. You've got to bless those that curse you.

You know, sometimes when we get behind a persons' back we can bless them out. We can chew them up. We can talk about them. The Lord says that when you get behind the back of your enemy, say something good about them. Bless those who do you evil, who persecute you and say all manner of evil things against you falsely. Don't get angry with them. Now you've put yourself in a position to hit a homerun!

In order for you to hit a homerun you've got to have something thrown at you (the ball). You can't hit a homerun with an easy, slow ball thrown to you. You have to have something thrown hard at you. They say the harder they throw it, the further you can knock it over the fence.

You've got to have some opposition. You're building character here and you're going to have some opposition because the devil is gonna try and knock you out! If you're on God's team the gates of hell will come up against you, but you're gonna win anyhow. You've got some opposition.

What kind of opposition do you have? Opposition in life comes in many forms. Sometimes it comes in criticism. Some folks will say: "He's alright, but…" There's always a 'but' in the way. "He would do alright, but he's got this little problem here". You're gonna have to learn that opposition comes in criticism.

Not only that, but opposition comes in having hard times. Sometimes you can't make ends meet. Can I get a witness? Sometimes everything comes due at the same time. Before you get this paid something else is due or something will break down. Hard times.

Hard times can't stop you from

growing. Hard times can't stop you from progressing. If you're on God's team, the harder the times, the further you can knock the ball over the fence.

Opposition will come up on everyone. Don't get angry when opposition shows up. Don't get angry when criticism comes. So many times when somebody is criticized they go and take a seat in the dugout. The dugout is where people become spectators and not participators.

Somebody will make you mad and you'll go home, sit down and say: "I'll show them! I wonder if they think they can make it without me?" I'll tell you this; you better stay on the team. Better stay on the field. Because if you don't stay on the team and on the field you won't have no pay when payday comes!

Judgment day is coming, and God is

going to call the workers. If you're not working when He comes there won't be no pay!

Don't go to the dugout. Stay on the field. If your enemies keep talking about you and doing you wrong, thank God for them. All they're doing is keeping you on your knees praying. These are God's rules and there is no changing them.

Now if you're playing on God's team, go to Him for your uniform. What He will give you is a belt of truth, a breastplate of righteousness, some boots of peace, a shield of faith, the helmet of salvation and the sword of the Spirit which is the word of God.

Once you've got on God's uniform the devil can't touch you. When you go to bat for God, some folks are going to think that you're crazy. There will be

times you may feel that you're all alone,
you're not. What you've got to do is go
ahead and do your job which is to get
on first base.

There are different ways for you to
get to first base. You can get a hit. You
can draw a walk or you can be hit by a
pitch. When you get hit by a pitch you
can drop your bat and go to first base.
Back in the book of Isaiah it says: "He
was bruised for me". And He didn't say
a mumbling word.

I used to wonder how He could do
that, but He knew that if He were to get
back at folks He would never hit a
homerun. When you're bruised they're
only knocking you nearer to home
plate.

When you're bruised, when you're
talked about, when you're mistreated
and when you're having a hard time,

you don't have to worry. You can drop your bat and walk to first base because can't nobody beat God teaching.

Licks that we should have gotten, Jesus took them and didn't say a mumbling word. He knew that every lick would get Him closer to home plate. So you stay, stay on God's team. God will make a way for you.

I'll tell you another thing. There is no batter like the one I'm going to tell you about. The most feared person in the batting order is the homerun hitter. He has the ability to change the outcome of the game with one swing of his bat. The homerun hitter I want to tell you about is Jesus, my pinch hitter; the homerun hitter with a bloody bat!

There is no greater hitter than the one I'm talking about. Whenever mankind gets in a pinch and can't see or make it's way out, all they have to do is call in the pinch hitter; Jesus. He can hit a curveball. He can hit a fastball. He can hit a spitball or a knuckleball. I don't care what kind of pitch you throw, Jesus can hit it. When you get in a tight spot and can't see your way out, call Jesus.

In the game of life the devil is on every side of you. Call on Jesus. He will help you overcome your problems. He's your pinch hitter and I'll tell you He's a homerun hitter!

I know that I'm right, but let me tell you about one game. Jesus and His disciples were on the sea one day and a storm came up. The wind was blowing and water was getting into the boat. The disciples were afraid that they were going to sink.

They were about to lose the game

against nature so they cried out: "Master wake up lest we perish!" And Jesus got up, walked to the front of the boat and all He said was: "Peace, be still." The wind hushed her mouth and didn't say another mumbling word. The waves smothered into a calm. Peter looked around and said: "What kind of man is this?" Well I'll tell you.....He's a homerun hitter!

Nature had to calm down when Jesus got up and spoke. They were in a tight situation, but Jesus knocked them home safely.

In this game you will either be a spectator; one who sits and watches, or you will be a participator; an active player in the game. If you're a player there are only two teams to play on; the devil's team or God's team. And if you're a spectator you're really a player and don't know it. You've already chosen a team.

If you're a player on Satan's team let me introduce you to your teammates. Starting in your outfield you have; HATE-LF, JEALOUSY-RF, IRRITATION-CF. The infield; DOUBT-1B, POVERTY-2B, TRIALS & TRIBULATIONS-3B, CRITICISM-SS, TIME-P and DEATH-C. The fellow in the black suit, behind home plate, that's JUSTICE, he's the UMPIRE. He's gonna call the play. This is Satan's team and I must say you have some hell of a teammates!

To play on God's team you've got to bring three things to the game. First you've got to bring an attitude and will to win. You may have some setbacks, but keep pushing onward. The only way you can lose is if you quit. There are no quitters on God's team.

Second, you've got to have some knowledge of the game. You've got to know your limitations. Know what you can and cannot say or do. Where you can and cannot go. God's team doesn't say or do any and everything. And they don't go everywhere.

Finally you've got to play by God's rules. Pray without ceasing. Believe that God's grace is sufficient and love your enemies.

When you came to bat and if you made it to first base you've just reached salvation. You must be saved to be on God's team. Now a lot of people think that once they're saved they're home free and don't have to do anything else. WRONG! There's still work to do.

Being on first base is fine, but you haven't scored any runs yet. However if you continue to do God's will and spread His word you will make it around the bases and score.

Remember when you first went to bat for God and you felt all alone out there? Well let me tell you this, Jesus has some teammates for you.

They are; LOVE, JOY, PEACE, LONGSUFFERING, GENTLENESS, GOODNESS, FAITH, MEEKNESS and TEMPERANCE. You've got plenty of help.

You're on first base and Doubt is saying: "You can't make it!" But Faith says: "Yes you can. Just hold on. Because without faith it is impossible to please God!" Poverty hollers over from second base: "You're broke, you've got nothing. You don't even have bread to eat!" But Faith says: "My God is rich and He will provide. Man shall not live by bread alone, but by every word of God. I've been a young man, I've been an old man, but I've never seen the righteous forsaken or His seed begging for bread. In my Father's house there are many mansions and He's got a place for me!"

Criticism says people are talking about you. Trials and Tribulations are showing you hard times. People are lying on you. They are cheating and stealing from you. But guess what? Just when things are really looking rough and you're really down, but not out, this is when you call for your pinch hitter. This is when Jesus comes to bat for you.

When Jesus stepped up to the plate old Time says: "This ain't nobody! I done got Abraham out. I got Jacob out and Jesus is going out too!" But Death hollers out: "Time shut up! You didn't get Abraham and Jacob, I did! I've got them right now here in the grave!"

They just didn't know who they were messing with when Jesus came to bat. I tell you He's a homerun hitter! This is the man who walked onto the deck of a boat in the midst of a storm and said: "Peace, be still" and the storm shut up. He's the one who said: "Lazarus come forth" and Lazarus got up from the grave. This man had power in His voice. These were games in the regular season.

In another regular season game a woman caught in the act of adultery was brought before Jesus. She wasn't brought there for her crime, but because the men who brought her were looking for a reason to criticize Jesus. You know, to be in God's plan you're *gonna have to act like Jesus.*

These men wanted to trap Him. They said the law says she is to be stoned, what do you say? When people want to trap you they put the Bible on you. They were trying to trick Jesus.

They wanted Him to say: "Stone her" so they could accuse Him and ask: "How can this man be talking about love one day and then want to kill someone the next?"

If He would have said: "Don't stone her" they would have said: "Look. He's going against the word of God!" But I tell you He's a homerun hitter! You can't get Him out because He knows how to bat.

Jesus being who He is just knelt down and began writing on the ground. My Pastor says He wrote the first time because it was a dirty conversation.

Some folks are always bringing up something dirty. When they bring up something dirty it's because they don't want to work. They want to start something. They want to get people arguing, fussing and fighting. You can't work, fussing and fighting at the same time.

However the men kept on pressing Jesus for an answer. Jesus kept on writing on the ground. They were saying: "Master, wake up now and tell us something. We're tithers in the church. We give our money every week and we got a right to know what you're gonna do!"

Jesus knows everything. So I'm thinking that He wrote the name of a woman, in another city. And when the oldest man looked down and saw his name down there Jesus looked up and said: "Now you who is without sin, cast the first stone!"

The old man turned and walked away. Then one by one, first the older men; the deacons and elders walked away and then the young men. They all walked away.

Here they were ready to kill somebody for something that they were guilty of themselves. The devil will get us to do that if we let him. You can't play on God's team unless you love people the way Jesus loves them.

Besides, if the woman was caught in adultery, where was the man? Adultery is not an act she could have done alone. Jesus asked the woman: "Where are your accusers?" She said: "I have none Lord". He said: "Neither do I condemn you. Go and sin no more".

These were games in the regular

season, but now He's playing in the World Series. Jesus stepped up to the plate and Time threw Him a fastball. Jesus hit it. They say the harder it's thrown, the further you can hit it. And that's how it should be with God's team. The harder things are thrown at us, the further we should be able to knock it back!

If the devil tells you don't speak to so and so because they've been talking about you, speak anyway. Greet them with a smile and ask how they've been doing. If you're on God's team the gates of hell can't prevail against you.

Jesus started around the bases. He knocked down Doubt at first base and said: "Without faith it is impossible to please God!" Went on around to second base and tied up Poverty telling him: "My God is rich and He will supply all my needs!" He went on to third base and knocked over Trials and Tribulations and told him: "All things work together for good. Trials workout for your good. Tribulations will work out for your good. Just hold on!"

He went into home plate, going so fast. He stirred up so much dust and Justice couldn't call the play. No he couldn't. There was so much dust everywhere. They said: "Justice is He out?" Justice said: "I don't know, but I heard Him say: "If you kill me, I'll rise. If you crucify me, I'll get up on the third day!"

Justice said: "I don't know if He's out or not. I can't determine it right now. I'm gonna call the play, but give me some time".

All night Friday, Justice couldn't call the play. All day gloomy Saturday,

Justice couldn't call the play. But early Sunday morning Justice didn't have to call the play. Early Sunday morning God called the play. He got up off His throne in Glory and saw 'THE ROCK' laying in a rock and got Him up! Justice didn't have to do anything. God called the play. God got Him up.

Jesus got up out of His grave clothes. The grave clothes were just wrapped around Him. He didn't unwrap them. He had a powerful body. He just got up and the grave clothes just collapsed. When the grave clothes collapsed the angels brought Him a new robe and then He got up out of the grave.

The Bible says that when He got up all the saints got up with Him. First to get up was Abraham; Father of the Faithful. Abraham said: Wait a minute,

I've got to wake up Jacob. Jacob! Jacob get up! The Lord done hit a homerun! Get up!"

Jacob got up, but said: "Hold it. I've got to wake up my twelve sons. I've got to wake up Joseph. I've got to wake up Rueben and Gad and Manasses. I've got to wake up all of my sons!"

And as each son got up they said: "Wait. Hold on just a few minutes. I've got 12,000 that I've got to get up". In the Book of Revelations John saw all of them.

John, what did you see? "I saw all of them. I saw 12,000 coming from Rueben. I saw 12,000 coming from Manasses. In other words I saw 12 times 12,000. I saw 144,000 that were going up to get their reward.

Wait a minute John, don't you see somebody else? The 144,000 came from the twelve tribes of Israel. The Gentiles weren't in that group. Just then it was as if God had pushed a button and changed the channel like it was on TV.

Then John said: "Wait a minute. I see a number, a number that no man can number". That's the crowd that you're in. That's the crowd that I'm in. That's the Gentile crowd. That number that no man could number, that's the crowd that we're in. That crowd was coming out of great trials and tribulations.

They had passed third base. If you ain't had no trials and tribulations you may not be in that number. You've got to have had some trials. You've got to have been talked about and mistreated to be in this number.

This group is on it's way home

because Jesus hit a homerun on Calvary with a bloody bat. It was more than 714, more than 715, more than 755 and more than 762. It was a number that no man could number. His hands were bloody. His head was bloody. His feet were bloody. His side was bloody. His back was bloody. This blood is what knocked us home! This blood cleaned us up and washed away our sins. I tell you, He's a homerun hitter, with a bloody bat!

Some folks might say: "When I see Jesus I'm gonna tell Him how you talked about me and mistreated me." if that's what you think then you might not be seeing Him. Jesus ain't having no tattletales or gossipers in His presence.

When we see Him we best be saying: "Thank you, thank you, thank you. For you've brought me from a mighty long way!" When your soul is saved you want to say "Thank you". You don't have anymore hate, no more jealousy, no more irritation.

Those people playing in the devil's outfield won't make it. If you play according to God's rules no devil or demon anywhere can stand against you. Just stay on the team. God will bring the victory. If you believe that you ought to say "Amen" and give God a hand.

Maybe there is someone out there right now who doesn't want to be a spectator any longer. Maybe you want to get on God's team today. Jesus said: "I stand at the door and knock; if any man hear my voice and open the door, I will come in and sup with him and he with me."

Do you hear Him knocking? If you do, why not open the door? This is how you get on the team. This is how you get to first base. You've got to get to first base in order for Jesus to drive you home. Don't wait until tomorrow because it's not promised to you.

Young men. Here's a story about a little boy named Johnny. Johnny was playing with his toys out in front of his house one day. An eighteen wheeler, a big, old tractor trailer truck came speeding down the street out of control. The truck struck Johnny and dragged him for a block before the driver could get it stopped.

They rushed Johnny to the hospital and into emergency surgery where a team of five doctors worked on him all night. They finally got him stabilized and placed him in the intensive care unit with another little boy named Michael.

When Johnny finally woke up he was in a lot of pain so Michael called for a nurse to bring Johnny some pain medication. After the nurse left Michael called over to Johnny and asked him his name and how he felt. Johnny told him his name and said that he was feeling really bad. Michael told Johnny to just hold on until tonight. He said every night around midnight Jesus makes His rounds in the hospital and He would stop by to see him.

Johnny said: "You know Michael, I've been a really bad boy. I've disobeyed mama, not done my chores and been bad in school. I've done so much wrong and I don't think Jesus wants to see me!"

Michael said: "At midnight if you

hold up your hand Jesus will come by." Johnny said: "Do you really think He will?" Michael answered: "Just hold up your hand and He will come by."

It was getting close to midnight and Michael saw Johnny trying to raise his hand, but being so weak from surgery he couldn't keep it up. So Michael got out of his bed and went over to Johnny's bed, took some pillows and propped up Johnny's hand so that it would stay up and went back to his bed.

Early the next morning Michael looked over and saw Johnny with his hand still up. He called to him, but got no answer. He got up and went to Johnny's bed to wake him, but Johnny had passed during the night.

Jesus had come by and put Johnny on His team and sent him home. All because that little boy believed, had faith and put his hand up to call on Jesus, he didn't have to lay there in pain and suffer any longer.

Johnny had become an All Star on God's team just because of his faith in Jesus. If you want Jesus to stop by and visit you today all you've got to do is hold up your hand. Anybody want on God's team today?

There might be somebody who needs Jesus to make a house call. Somebody might be weary, tired and worn out. All you've got to do is hold up your hand. Maybe you're tired of fussing at your children. The more you talk, the worse they get. Hold up your hand. Jesus wants to come by your house.

There might be someone out there saying: "I'm tired of trying to make ends meet! It seems the harder I try, the worse things become!" Hold up *your hand!*

Someone might be saying: "I'm tired of aches and pains!" Hold your hand up! Somebody might be lonely, but you don't have to be alone. Someone may have cried last night. Somebody may have been beaten and abused or molested. All you have to do is hold up your hand.

Somebody may be sick today. Hold it up! If you've tried to make somebody understand and they won't understand all you've got to do is hold up your hand like Johnny did.

If you're weak and frail you ought to hold your hand up. If you've been lied on and talked about, hold your hand up. If you've been put out, hold your hand up. If at times your job gets to be too much for you, hold your hand up. He's coming by!

I want you to think about this: Has He been to your house? Will He stop by? Have you ever been down to your last dime and Jesus stepped in right on time?

You've probably been to church and had the preacher ask God to get your child right. Forget the preacher. God is not a respecter of persons or titles. Ask God yourself! Stop talking and put your hand up. You don't have to put your physical hand up, but in your heart put your hand up. God reads your heart. He'll stop by.

I realize that this sounds like a sermon; that's because it is. It really doesn't matter because the message is still the same, I don't care how or where you get it. To some this may be the only time they are told exactly how it is. It's been put before you so that you shouldn't have any problem understanding it.

What it all comes down to is this: You've got to be on one team or the other. The choice is yours, so why not join God's team and be a winner? Jesus guarantees the victory. If He's with you, He's more than the whole world against you. Who wouldn't want to play with a teammate like that?

Enough preaching. Men, it's time for you to take your position as the head of the household. Stop letting these women prop you up. It's your job to lead. However if you lead in the wrong direction you will be held accountable for what you've done or failed to do. As the head, you're like the leadoff batter. Your job is to get on first base. If you do this, the rest of the family should follow. Jesus is waiting to drive you *home. Play ball!*

The Conversion From Player To Real Man

Let's get back to the Barber Shop

The Conversion: Player To Real Man

Hopefully after reading this, a few of you Players out there may desire to try and change your lifestyle and upgrade your way of living. If you feel that you can't make the changes to become a real man there are only a few reasons not to try.

One: You're afraid of trying and failing. If that's the case all you have to do is pull yourself back up and try again.

Two: You've never seen a real man and don't know what you're supposed to be doing. I find this really hard to believe, that you've never seen a real man.

Three: You're sorry as hell and

you're content with where you are in life.

For those of you who want to make a change, start by taking inventory of yourself. Take a hard look at you and how you're living. Set a goal for yourself and then make a plan to get to where you want to be. Be realistic, it's not going to happen overnight. It took years to get to where you are now. Hopefully it won't take as long to get you where you want and desire to be. You have to lose that Player mentality if there really is such a thing. Personally I think that's a game that you guys are playing with your own minds. As long as this game is going on in your mind you will always feel that you can 't lose. The time will come when you realize that you have lost at this game of life, but it will be too late. You'll probably be real old, bent over, in a wheelchair, using a cane or worse. No income, no companions and a very dark and bleak outlook for the rest of your days!

Look at your children, if there are any that you know of. See what, if there is anything you can do for them at this stage in their lives.

Apologize to and check on the mother, if she'll hear it. After all, you probably left her holding the bag when it came to the children. How can you ever make up for all the heartache you caused and the dollars she spent on you and all you ever did was go to another woman?

She remembers the many nights that she spent taking care of a sick child and you were nowhere to be found. You were probably out at a club having yourself a good old time.

Maybe you were just down the block with the boys turning up your '40'. Either way you weren't there to share in the responsibilities of raising the children. Take a deep breath, it may not be too late to be a contributor in the lives of your children.

Get yourself a job and keep a lookout for an opportunity that will propel you to a higher station in life. Search for that ladder that you'll need to climb for success in your life.

When you find that ladder check and see how narrow it is. Very little room for mistakes. "A man has got to know his limitations".* Like I said before: "Everybody that comes with you can't go with you!" Not enough room there for you to bring your buddies along.

* Clint Eastwood- 'Magnum Force'

Neither you nor the ladder can carry all that weight. You best let them find their own ladder. I'm not going to tell you, but I hope that you know who all your faith and trust needs to go to. He didn't bring you this far to leave you.

So what you gonna do? You gonna pee or get off the pot? I told you before, Players ain't got no need to even be on the pot because they ain't gonna do anything anyway. You've got to break away from those guys so that you can live. You must be a man to truly live and not merely exist.

Stop being a taker and start being a giver. Give of your money, of yourself and of your time. However I want you to know that the power company only wants money. They don't want you or your time, just money.

You fathers, don't think that just

because you can't provide financial support at this time that you should give up and not see or spend time with your children. They don't want your money. They want your acknowledgement. They want you in their lives.

Let's be real about this situation, especially you mothers. If the father hasn't been supporting the children all this time, then you withholding visitation with the children doesn't do anyone any good especially the children.

The children were being fed and clothed without his support before and they will continue to be provided for. Whatever the father can add to the pot will only enhance or enrich their lives. It may make things a little better and easier for them.

Mothers, back off and let this used

to be Player wanting to be a man try and establish himself on that highway to becoming a real man and a daddy.

When it's all over I wish, hope and pray for the best for all of you; men and Players alike. If you have found one thing in these pages that can help you or point you in a direction that will improve your station in life, then I've done something good.

If not, I haven't failed because it's on you to do the right thing. So let me leave you with this: Don't let the cost of being a man be too high for you!

Epilogue

Well gentlemen there you have it. Real men should not have any problems with what has been said here. Players on the other hand may not like what was said and may not agree with it. Those are their opinions and they are entitled to them.

If you call yourself a Player and you haven't picked up on anything here then that's on you. If at the end of the day you find yourself seeking refuge at some woman's house just so you'll have a place to lay your head, then you haven't learned anything.

If you think that is the best that you can do, then you really have a low opinion of yourself and only you can change that.

If you think that woman is allowing you to lay up there because you're so good in bed....get real. Don't believe your own hype! You're only a legend in your own mind! You're not that good!   Players, you just keep on playing the game. Real men, you don't have to worry about them. Every time the Player tries to step into your 'game' or way of life all you have to do is change the rules. He can't keep up. After all, how can he possibly know where you're coming from if he doesn't know where you've been or where you're going?   When all is said and done, a man is going to be a man, but a real man is going to be somebody!   Now I'll ask the question again: "How can you be a man if you've never seen or met a man?" I hope you've found an answer in here.